Major Competitive Reality Shows:
America's Got Talent

Jim Whiting

Mason Crest Publishers
Philadelphia

Mason Crest Publishers
370 Reed Road
Broomall, PA 19008
www.masoncrest.com

CPSIA Compliance Information: Batch #060110-MCRS. For further
information, contact Mason Crest Publishers at 1-866-MCP-Book

First printing
1 3 5 7 9 8 6 4 2

Library of Congress Cataloging-in-Publication Data

Whiting, Jim, 1943-
  Major competitive reality shows: America's got talent / Jim Whiting.
      p. cm. — (Major competitive reality shows)
  Includes bibliographical references and index.
  ISBN 978-1-4222-1670-5 (hc)
  ISBN 978-1-4222-1933-1 (pb)
  1. America's got talent (Television program)—Juvenile literature. I. Title.
  PN1992.77.A5625W45 2010
  791.45'72—dc22
                              2010015969

Photo credits: AP/Wide World Photos: cover, 10, 24, 28, 31, 32; Getty Images: 16, 36, 39;
Library of Congress: 8; used under license from Shutterstock, Inc.: 1, 4, 13, 18, 19, 34, 38;
www.youtube.com: 41.

Contents

1

By 2007, Terry Fator was ready to give up on his dream of show-business success. However, Terry's appearance that year on the show *America's Got Talent* turned his professional fortunes around. Terry impressed the show's judges and audience. His victory earned him a $1 million prize, as well as a chance to become a star entertainer in Las Vegas.

The Mega-Million Dollar Deal

One day in 2007, *ventriloquist* Terry Fator walked onto the stage in a thousand-seat theater at a fair in Dallas. This was something he had done hundreds of times previously, often under less than ideal conditions. "Fairs would stick me on a little stage in the back of a fair and have me do three shows in the hottest part of the afternoon," he later recalled.

On this day, there was exactly one person in the audience, a 12-year-old boy. Though he was discouraged by the meager turnout, Fator began his act. Soon a few teenagers trickled in. Fator got his hopes up. Maybe it was the start of something.

It was, but not in the way he wanted. The teens were members of the cleaning crew. After a few minutes, they started folding up the rows of empty chairs.

READY TO QUIT

For Fator, that dismal performance was the last straw. He was 41, he had been performing for nearly his entire adult life, and now he couldn't even attract a decent crowd. "I called my wife and said, 'I don't want to do this anymore,'" he said.

Just over a year later, however, Fator signed a contract to appear for five years at the Mirage Hotel in Las Vegas, Nevada. The contract Terry signed in May 2008 was worth $100 million, with a five-year option worth another $100 million. The Mirage even named the arena in which he would perform in his honor—the Terry Fator Theatre.

The working conditions were a little different too. At one time, Terry had to buy his own bottled water when he got thirsty. When he asked for a snack to keep up his strength, stagehands growled, "Get your own dang fruit tray." He slept in cheap motels. After signing his large contract, though, Terry was provided with all the *amenities* a top performer could expect. What happened to account for this rags-to-riches transformation? *America's Got Talent.*

GETTING A SECOND CHANCE AT SUCCESS

When Terry called his wife after the Texas disaster, she calmed him down. Then she suggested that he try out for the second season of *America's Got Talent.* Produced and developed by Simon Cowell, the famous *American Idol* judge, the show had made a very successful debut in June 2006. Fator agreed, but as he told journalist Sony Hocklander, he didn't expect much to happen:

> **"Not in my wildest dreams did I imagine I would win that show. Essentially I auditioned because the guy that was the ventriloquist the first season got on [Late Night with David Letterman]. . . . So I figured I'd do three episodes like he did and end up on David Letterman."**

Fator did much better than simply lasting for three episodes, though. He kept advancing until he reached the finals. On August 21,

2007, Terry was revealed as the winner of the competition. Throughout the season, Terry won the admiration of Simon and the other judges. Terry later commented:

> **"Simon Cowell said I was one of the top two entertainers on the planet. . . . And getting a compliment from Simon Cowell, well, not many people get a compliment like that."**

The association with Cowell is one reason *America's Got Talent* was a success right from the beginning. Another reason is that it taps into a long tradition of similar variety programs in the United States.

START OF A LONG TRADITION

This tradition began in 1934 when *Major Bowes Amateur Hour* debuted on WHN radio in New York City. This program was originated by Edward Bowes, a theatrical producer who had been a military officer. The show soon became a hit. It reached a national audience after moving to the CBS radio network in 1936. One reason for its popularity was the audience participation format. The show would receive up to 20,000 calls an hour as listeners voted for their favorite performers.

The program launched the careers of a number of performers. Perhaps the most successful was Frank Sinatra. In 1935 he appeared on *Major Bowes Amateur Hour* as part of a singing group called the Hoboken Four. They won the competition, and received a six-month contract to perform on stage and radio across the United States. Other contestants who went on to

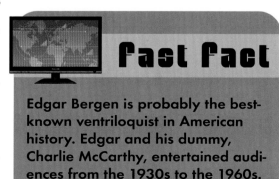

Fast Fact

Edgar Bergen is probably the best-known ventriloquist in American history. Edgar and his dummy, Charlie McCarthy, entertained audiences from the 1930s to the 1960s.

national notice included opera singers Lily Pons, Beverly Sills, and Robert Merrill.

Bowes died in 1946. His assistant Ted Mack kept the show going, eventually changing the name to *Ted Mack and the Original Amateur Hour*. In 1948, Mack expanded the show's range by putting it on television, where it quickly became one of the most popular programs. The radio show ended in 1952, while the television program ran until 1970.

OTHER INFLUENCES

Another important influence was *The Ed Sullivan Show*. Host Ed Sullivan had been a sports reporter and entertainment writer before the television show aired on CBS in June 1948. *The Ed Sullivan Show* ran until 1971, making it the longest-running variety show in television history. *The Ed Sullivan Show* was one of the top-rated television programs of its era.

Television entertainer Ed Sullivan (center) was credited with helping to launch many careers among the more than 10,000 acts that appeared on his show. Among the most famous performers who appeared were Elvis Presley and The Beatles (pictured). Ed Sullivan also gave dozens of African-American performers national exposure at a time when there were few other opportunities for them.

Elements of the *Amateur Hour* format were revived in 1976 with The Gong Show. This program featured three celebrity judges who would bang on a gong when they were particularly displeased with an act. Rules for using the gong varied, but the judges would often milk the gag for all it was worth, getting up slowly and edging over to the large gong as the audience waited in anticipation.

In 1992, television weatherman Willard Scott revived the concept on the Family Channel, calling his show *The New Original Amateur Hour*. Though the show achieved good ratings, it was canceled after a single year. One of the highlights of this show was the debut of Backstreet Boy Nick Carter, who was just 12 at the time.

In the late 1990s, reality television programs and game shows began to become more popular in the United States. Cowell's program *American Idol* became a huge hit when it debuted in 2002. This success opened the way for many new reality shows, including *America's Got Talent*.

2

AGT Gets off the Ground

With the phenomenal success of *American Idol,* the show's co-producer, Simon Cowell, wanted to develop similar programs that would allow talented people to showcase themselves. In 2004 he created a show called *X-Factor.* This singing competition tried to identify singers with the types of talents that could lead to stardom. Early in 2006 he premiered *American Inventor.* This program looked for people with interesting ideas that might one day become useful products.

While making those two shows, Simon had also been working on an idea he called *Britain's Got Talent.* The program was originally scheduled to debut in the fall of 2005. A well-known British media personality named Paul O'Grady was supposed to be the host. However, the show's producers could not come to terms with ITV, the Brititsh network that was going to carry the program. The show had to be put on hold.

Simon had already been planning an American version of the show. When the British program was put on hold, he focused on the

American program. Early in 2006 Simon announced that *America's Got Talent* would premiere that summer. During a press conference, he made it clear what he was looking for:

> **"You can be 2 years old, 100 years old. You can be the next Destiny's Child, you can be the next Jackson 5 or you can be the next David Copperfield. This is a show literally open to anybody."**

Like *American Idol,* a panel of three judges would make the original decisions about which contestants moved on to successive rounds. The final winner would be determined by a nationwide vote by viewers. Original plans called for the winner to receive a $1 million contract to perform in Las Vegas. With the possibility of a child winning the competition, the prize was changed to a $1 million payoff.

A HOST AND JUDGES

One of the first questions about the new show involved the host. This is the person who would fill the same role that Ryan Seacrest does for *American Idol.* The answer wasn't long in coming. It would be Regis Philbin, one of the most popular and best-known people in show business. Though he was 74 at the time of his selection, Regis appeared to have the energy of a much younger man. He was excited to be involved with the new show, telling reporters:

> **"For years I've thought about hosting a variety show on television but I could never put it together in my mind. Finally, here it is and I'm thrilled to be a part of it."**

In a way, Regis Philbin was a perfect symbolic choice. From 1999 to 2002 he had been host of the popular game show *Who Wants to Be a Millionaire?* This program had been so successful when it debuted in the summer of 1999 that it helped to inspire the creation of other reality-

According to the *Guinness Book of World Records*, Regis Philbin has spent more time in front of a television camera than anyone else in history—nearly 17,000 hours.

style game shows and competitions, including *American Idol* and *America's Got Talent.*

Simon Cowell would have been an obvious choice for one of the three judges. However, his contract with *American Idol* prevented him from serving as a judge on *America's Got Talent.* Instead, three people with longstanding connections to the entertainment industry were chosen as judges. One was Piers Morgan, a British newspaper editor and television personality. Another was American actor David Hasselhoff, who was best known for his starring roles in the hit television shows *Knight Rider* (aired 1982 to 1986) and *Baywatch* (aired 1989 to 2001). The third was R&B singer and actress Brandy Norwood.

AUDITIONS GET UNDERWAY

Auditions began in Los Angeles during early April 2006, and continued later that month in Chicago, New York, and Atlanta. The show's first episode aired June 21, 2006, on NBC. It was an immediate hit. More than 12 million people tuned in, making it the evening's most-watched program. The numbers even exceeded the audience for the 2002 debut of *American Idol.*

From the beginning, it was evident that all kinds of performers were represented. The acts that were quickly rejected included a break-dancer dressed as a cow who squirted milk at the judges, a voice impersonator whose imitations were terrible, an off-key opera singer, and a man who tried to play music using a saw.

Performers who advanced included a woman who shot a bow and arrow using her feet while standing on her hands, a musician who used different parts of his body to play horns, and Bobby Von Merta, who appeared as Bobby Badfingers. Billed as the world's fastest fingersnapper, Badfingers added dancing to his performance and received a standing ovation.

Piers Morgan

Piers Morgan was born in 1965 in Newick, England. He began his professional career as a newspaper reporter and columnist.

When Piers was just 28 years old, he was named editor of *News of the World.* He was one of the youngest people to ever head a major newspaper. He left his position within two years, becoming editor of the *Daily Mirror,* one of England's largest newspapers. However, Piers was fired from this job in 2004 over publication of photos from the Iraq War that were proven to have been fake.

In 2006 Piers became editorial director of a new weekly newspaper, *First News.* It presents world news to children aged 7 through 14. *First News* currently has a circulation of more than 750,000.

Piers has also done extensive television work in both the United Kingdom and the United States. In 2008 he won *Celebrity Apprentice.* He has also written eight books. Three of these have been **memoirs**.

Piers was married for 17 years but divorced in 2008. He has three children.

THE TOP TEN

As weeks went by, the judges determined which performers would be dropped from the show and which ones could keep going. Finally, the ten finalists were selected. The acts represented the diversity of talent Simon Cowell had wanted for *America's Got Talent.* The first-season finalists included:

- 73-year-old Vivian Smallwood, who performed hip-hop songs under the nickname Rappin' Granny;
- 11-year-old singer/guitarist Bianca Ryan;
- At Last, a four-man hip-hop group that sang without musical accompaniment;
- David & Dania, a pair of magicians who performed a bewildering array of almost instantaneous costume changes;
- All That, a five-man clogging group;
- Taylor Ware, a yodeler;
- Jon & Owen, juggler/comedians whose act included performing with lighted torches;
- Celtic Spring, an Irish-American family dance and fiddle band;
- Realis, a man and woman who performed acrobatic dances; and
- The Millers, two brothers who sang while playing guitar and harmonica.

The top three were Bianca Ryan, All That, and the Millers. On August 17, 2006, Bianca was named the winner of the first season.

OFF TO A GREAT START

From her first appearance on *America's Got Talent,* Bianca had made a powerful impression on the judges. When the Philadelphia native strode confidently onto the stage for her audition, she told the judges, "My dream is to be a famous singer and hopefully have my own TV show and not just 15 minutes of fame."

Simon Cowell announces that 12-year-old singing sensation Bianca Ryan has signed a contract with Columbia Records, September 2006. Bianca won the first season of *America's Got Talent*.

Brandy was skeptical when Bianca announced she would sing the song "And I Am Telling You I'm Not Going," from the musical *Dreamgirls*. The song requires a singer with a powerful voice. The small preteen did not look like she could do it justice. But moments after Ryan began her *rendition*, Brandy was on her feet, along with the rest of the audience. "That was unbelievable," Brandy said when Ryan finished. "You are my favorite contestant in this competition."

Since winning the $1 million prize on *America's Got Talent*, Bianca has released several albums and gone on tour.

3

Making Changes

Even before *America's Got Talent* premiered in the summer of 2006, NBC executives planned to air a second season in the following January. During the fall and winter months, many more people watch television. However, the network changed its mind. Moving to January would place the show in direct competition with *American Idol*, which was an established hit on the Fox network. In addition, NBC felt confident that by airing *AGT* during the summer months, the show would maintain the high ratings it had established during its first season.

The show did experience several major changes before the second season aired. One was that Regis Philbin reluctantly decided to leave as host. His popular morning program *Live with Regis and Kelly* was based in New York City. *America's Got Talent* was taped in Los Angeles. Regis felt that frequent travel between the two cities would be too difficult.

A NEW HOST
To replace the popular Regis, the producers turned to another well-known entertainment figure: Jerry Springer. Jerry had become famous

during the 1990s for his often-rowdy afternoon program, *The Jerry Springer Show.* The show became known for covering controversial topics. Flying chairs, screaming matches, and fights between guests occurred regularly.

Yet there was more to Jerry than most people knew. Television audiences got to learn more about Jerry when he appeared on *Dancing With the Stars* in the fall of 2006. Jerry, who is in his 60s, had a hard time keeping up with the other dancers, who were much younger. However, he made a favorable impression on the judges, and his personality helped keep him on the program for several weeks. Viewers realized that Jerry was nowhere near as bad as the reputation of his show made him out to be. One longtime friend noted:

> "Most of America only knows Jerry as the guy reacting to the insanity of his TV show guests. Now they're seeing the Jerry we know—the **self-effacing** and witty guy who's worlds away from what he's most famous for."

Jerry Springer served as mayor of Cincinnati and was an award-winning television news anchorman before his daytime talk show, *The Jerry Springer Show,* began airing in 1991. Jerry was hired as host of *America's Got Talent* for the show's second season.

Sharon Osbourne signs copies of her best-selling autobiography at a book store in London.

A NEW JUDGE

The second change was Brandy's departure from the show. The singer had originally planned to participate in the second season. However, in December 2006 she was involved in a car accident in which a woman was killed. The accident threw her life into turmoil. In April 2007, Brandy said that she would not return as a judge. The singer felt that she could not give the show the amount of attention it needed.

To replace her, Simon Cowell turned to Sharon Osbourne, the wife of legendary rock star Ozzy Ozbourne. Sharon had been involved in promoting her husband's music career for many years. Few people knew about her until MTV created a reality show about Ozzy Osbourne's family life. The show ran from 2002 to 2005 and made Sharon a celebrity as well.

Simon knew Sharon well. She had been a judge on his show *X-Factor* for four seasons. He liked and respected her. As an NBC executive noted,

"Sharon Osbourne is show business personified and she has seen and done it all. She will make an excellent fit with David and Piers, who we're delighted to have back for another great season."

A NEW FORMAT

A third major change to *America's Got Talent* involved the audition cities. For the second season, Dallas replaced Atlanta as one of four host cities for performers. The other three cities remained the same. Performers who were selected at the auditions were taken to Las Vegas for what was termed a "boot camp." There, they had a chance to work with experts in their areas of entertainment. This would give the *AGT* contestants additional polishing before they performed in further rounds of the series.

When the second season of *America's Got Talent* debuted in early June 2007, the ratings justified NBC's decision to air it in the summer. The program had clearly retained its popularity, especially among those in the *coveted* 18-49 age range. *America's Got Talent* drew nearly 13 million viewers for the premiere. It not only won its time slot, but also outperformed all other reality show premieres that season.

Viewers once again were treated to a wide variety of bizarre acts. The initial audition cuts included a Valley Girl rapper who mooned the judges, a *mime* who talked and sang, and a band that produced music by squeezing their hands together.

This season's ten finalists were far less diverse than had been the case in the first season. Only two—martial arts dance troupe Side Swipe and reggae-inspired dancers Calypso Tumblers—weren't singers or performers in which singing was a vital part of their acts. The other finalists included a family country band, The Duttons; stay-at-home dad Cas

Haley, a singer and guitar player; sewer worker Robert Hatcher; plus-sized singers/dancers The Glamazons; cruise ship performer Jason Pritchett; 14-year-old country singer Julienne Irwin; Butterscotch (Antoinette Clinton); and ventriloquist Terry Fator. Finally the voters narrowed the finalists down to two: Cas Haley and Terry Fator.

IT'S EITHER HIM OR ME

Terry's road to the finals hadn't been easy. When he walked on stage the first time, he had to combat the prejudices of the judges. "Oh, no, a ventriloquist," David Hasselhoff moaned. Sharon Osbourne later confessed, "When you came in, I thought, oh Lordie, Lord, not again." Piers Morgan was equally skeptical.

What the judges didn't realize at first was how different Terry was from other ventriloquists. In addition to throwing his voice, he could do impressions of many famous singers, using 15 different puppets that appeared to perform the vocals. His impressions were hilarious and right on target.

In his first appearance, Terry had his puppet Emma Taylor sing "At Last," the signature song of noted blues singer Etta James. As soon as the puppet crooned the first two words, Hasselhoff said "Wow!" and scrambled to his feet. Osbourne did the same thing. "I thought your act was absolutely brilliant," Hasselhoff added when Fator finished. Though he added a note of caution: "But to get to a million dollars, you gotta knock us out."

Fator proved up to the challenge. His subsequent performances were even better. "I take everything I said about ventriloquists back," Hasselhoff said at one point. "You are ready." In the finale, Hasselhoff showed how completely Fator had won him over:

"This competition is like a horse race and you're like the dark horse. And now on the outside comes Terry Fator, comin' in, comin' in. You know what, you're no longer the dark horse. Man, you are leadin' this competition. You're unbelievable, really. I mean, you've done Etta James, the Rat Pack, Tony Bennett, Louis Armstrong and you did a Garth Brooks better than Garth Brooks."

In his book *Who's the Dummy Now*, Fator described the agonizing 15 seconds after Springer said, "The winner of *America's Got Talent*, the winner of the title 'Best New Act in America,' and the winner of ONE MILLION DOLLARS is . . .":

"As I stood in front of America, my heart began to pound in a way I had never thought possible. I could feel it pulsing, pounding on my rib cage relentlessly, threatening to break through my chest at any moment. . . . Countless hopes and dreams were riding on the next two words. Would Jerry say 'Cas Haley' or my name? Finally, he said it: 'Terry Fator!'"

MAKING SIMON HAPPY

Simon Cowell thoroughly approved of the choice. As he told journalist Jim Halterman in 2008, "Everything changed last year on *Got Talent* when the guy who won, Terry Fator, this ventriloquist, went on to sign a $150 million contract with a Vegas casino. So, you know, the show actually did its job. It found a star."

Terry had been waiting a long time to be found. When the time came he was ready. He had worked hard to develop his act, he explained:

"I feel like I am the poster boy of the American dream. But it's not like winning the lottery—I earned it. I spent years and years **honing** my craft, working on it and learning to do it as well as I possibly could."

4

Continuing the Success

The *America's Got Talent* team—host Jerry Springer and judges Sharon Osbourne, Piers Morgan, and David Hasselhoff—returned for a third season in 2008. For this season's show, auditions were held in five cities: New York, Chicago, Los Angeles, Dallas, and Atlanta. In addition, those who wanted to compete on the show could submit videos through MySpace or Facebook. The result was more than 200,000 entries.

Viewers of the auditions—which were televised beginning in early June 2008—were treated to the usual goofiness: a barefoot woman who read poetry while jumping up and down on broken glass, a ventriloquist who couldn't keep his mouth closed, a man who made barnyard animal noises, and a host of terrible impersonators.

By the end of the audition period, more than 100 acts had been invited to Las Vegas. This number was soon *winnowed* to 40. These performers were given a three-week break so that NBC could broadcast the Summer Olympic games from Beijing, China. The extra time allowed the surviving acts to become even better.

STILL DRAWING BIG NUMBERS

The show's popularity continued. The early episodes of 2008 were attracting more than 14 million viewers. An advertising executive, Brad Adgate, said that those numbers were:

> "As good as many hits in the regular season. It's unusual because [*America's Got Talent* is] in its third year and shows tend to go the other way. This one is on an uptick."

The show's good ratings once again made NBC executives think about moving *America's Got Talent* to the regular fall/winter broadcasting season. However, ultimately the network decided not to mess with

The third-season finalists on *America's Got Talent* perform together. Pictured are (left to right) Paul Salos, Nuttin' But Stringz, Eli Mattson (on piano), Donald Braswell, Kaitlyn Maher (in front of piano), Queen Emily, Sarah Lenore, Neal Boyd, Joseph Hall, and The Wright Kids.

the show's success. Ben Silverman of NBC Entertainment explained, "We like it as an annual event in the summer." Simon Cowell added, "We've said no [to moving it]. Keep it as a summer show, separated from *Idol*. I don't think we'd ever want to divide the audience that way."

EVEN MORE SINGERS

In the third season, the finalists were even more singer-oriented. The only non-vocalists were brothers Damien and Tourie Escobar, who played violins and called themselves Nuttin' But Stringz. The other finalists included opera singers Neal Boyd and Donald Braswell, soul singer Queen Emily, Frank Sinatra impersonator Paul Salos, Elvis impersonator Joseph Hall, and pianist/singer Eli Mattson.

Two of the finalists—Kaitlyn Maher and the bluegrass singing group the Wright Kids—attracted attention because of their ages. The Wrights were 12, 9, and 6 years old, while Kaitlyn was just 4 years old. Simon told reporter Jim Halterman,

> **"Well, you know, we talk about this a lot. There's one argument that says we shouldn't be putting these kids on under the age of 16. I think you've got to take it case by case. I mean, on the show this year we've got a four year old. But I've got to tell you, this is the most mature, ambitious four year old I've ever met in my life and if we didn't put her on this show, she'd be entering something else."**

Neal Boyd—an insurance salesman and opera singer who performed the showpiece tenor ***aria*** "Nessun Dorma" (from Italian composer Giacomo Puccini's opera *Turandot*) in his audition and again in the finals—emerged as the victor. This aria seems to be a lucky song in the *Got Talent* series. Paul Potts had performed it on the way to winning the first season of a spinoff show, *Britain's Got Talent*, in 2007.

OVERCOMING OBSTACLES

Like Terry Fator, Neal Boyd's triumph ended a long struggle with adversity. Neal was raised by his single mother, who struggled to make ends meet. Overweight and biracial, Boyd was often bullied at school.

Surprisingly, his life-changing moment came when his brother was forced to do a school project on classical music. His brother brought home a CD called *The Three Tenors*, which featured three well-known opera singers. The album didn't impress his brother, but it had a profound impact on Neal. He later explained:

Sharon Osbourne

Sharon Osbourne was born in Brixton, England on October 9, 1952. Her father was music manager Don Arden. During the 1970s, one of Arden's clients was Black Sabbath. The rock group featured a lead vocalist named Ozzy Osbourne, who became known for his wild behavior. When the band fired Osbourne in 1979, Sharon began dating him and became his manager. Her father was outraged. He broke off contact with Sharon for over 20 years. Sharon and Ozzy were married in 1982. They have three children, Aimee, Jack, and Kelly.

Although Ozzy has been famous for many years, most people learned about Sharon because of the MTV reality show *The Osbournes*. The program, which depicted life in the Osbourne family home, ran from 2002 to 2005. It was one of MTV's most popular shows ever. Sharon also hosted a short-lived talk show and served as judge on the *X-Factor* during its first four seasons.

In 2002, Sharon was diagnosed with colon cancer. She was fortunate to detect the disease in its early stages and survived. Since then, she has become active in raising awareness of cancer and getting people to donate money to fight the disease.

Sharon has written two autobiographies. Her first, *Extreme*, was published in 2005 and won Biography of the Year at the British Book Awards. With more than 2 million copies sold, it is one of the most successful autobiographies by a woman ever published. Her second book, *Extreme, Survivor*, was published in 2007.

"The moment I heard Luciano Pavarotti, Placido Domingo, and José Carreras, they just blew me away. That day changed my heart. Even though they were singing operatic arias in languages like Italian and Spanish I realized that I didn't need to understand the words to understand the music."

That experience ignited Neal's enthusiasm for opera. He pursued his dream of singing through high school and college. In 2001, he gave a solo performance in New York's famous Carnegie Hall. He also became involved in many performances in his native Missouri, eventually becoming known as the "voice of Missouri."

HEARING FROM HIS HERO

It was especially fitting that one of the letters of congratulation after winning the competition came from Placido Domingo, who wrote:

"Congratulations Neal. By participating in *America's Got Talent*, you have brought to America's ears opera, so be proud of it. And I'm sure from today on that you are starting a brilliant career."

What Boyd hopes will indeed be a brilliant career continued with the release of his first CD, *My American Dream*, in June 2009.

5

Members of Acrodunk perform during the fourth season of *America's Got Talent*. The team members impressed the crowd by performing acrobatic basketball dunks set to music. They had previously appeared on *AGT*'s first season. Both times, however, Acrodunk was eliminated in the semifinals.

Even More Acts

The fourth season kicked off with a major change. Jerry Springer stepped down as host. Jerry had begun working with a theatre company during the summer of 2009, at the same time *America's Got Talent* would air. Along with the demands of filming *The Jerry Springer Show*, there just wasn't enough time to do anything else. Jerry said:

> "I've had a wonderful time serving as host on *America's Got Talent*. These last two seasons, working with everyone associated with the show and all the extraordinary and talented performers across America, has been an incredibly rewarding experience for me."

To replace him, producers tapped Nick Cannon. At 28 years old, Nick was younger than the previous two hosts had been. He had started his career as a stand-up comedian in Los Angeles when he was a teenager. Since then, Nick has acted in television and films, recorded a rap album and several singles, produced records, and served as on-air television host.

Calling his new position "the best summer job ever," Nick told MTV's Jocelyn Vena that he would be a terrific host:

> "I'm cut from the same cloth as all those contestants. I was an 8-year-old onstage at talent shows at churches. I can relate directly with all those contestants and I'm a fan of the show. . . . You have some of the wackiest people coming up to you. It's just hilarious. I just got to stand there and let the comedy flow."

EXPANDED AUDITIONS

As Nick Cannon noted, there was plenty of wackiness as the new season began. In 2009, auditions were held in nine cities: Atlanta, Boston, Chicago, Houston, Los Angeles, Miami, New York, Seattle, and Washington, D.C. A whopping 160 acts flew to Las Vegas for further polishing—though Cannon joked that 25 didn't even get out of the airport.

And as usual, many of the contestants maintained the show's reputation for zaniness. One man stuck sharp objects up his nose. A woman danced as a pink gorilla and removed part of her clothing while dancing. The "Indestructible Man" climbed a ladder made of swords. Another man sang about his love for David Hasselhoff.

BRING 'EM BACK

Though he wasn't officially a judge, in 2009 Simon Cowell became involved in the judging process. He said that too many good acts had been eliminated, and wanted to give some of them a second chance. As a result, two "wild card" acts were added during the following four weeks.

The field of contestants was finally narrowed down to ten finalists. This group of finalists was somewhat more varied than in the previous two seasons. There were four non-singing acts. They included breakdancer Hairo Torres; the Fab Five, a *quintet* of clogging sisters ranging

The three *America's Got Talent* judges watch the show's new host, Nick Cannon (center), on stage with season four finalists Lawrence Beamen (left) and Voices of Glory.

in age from 23 to 35 who were all wives and mothers; 75-year-old comedian Grandma Lee, who had turned to performing to cope with the death of her husband more than a decade earlier; and Recycled Percussion, four friends who used a variety of cast-off pieces of junk such as pots, pans, trashcans, and even chainsaws to create music.

The other six finalists included Voices of Glory, a group consisting of siblings Michael (age 17), Avery (13), and Nadia (9) Cole; opera singer Bárbara Padilla, a cancer survivor; the Texas Tenors, three young men who had formed their group less than a year earlier in the hope of appearing on *America's Got Talent*; singer/guitarists Kevin Skinner and

For winning the fourth season of *America's Got Talent*, country singer Kevin Skinner was given the opportunity to perform a show in Las Vegas. His first CD, *Long Ride*, was released on March 17, 2010.

Drew Stevyns; and Lawrence Beamen, whose deep, booming voice immediately impressed both the judges and the audience.

Padilla's performance in the finals nearly resulted in a repeat triumph for operatic singers, but Kevin Skinner emerged as the winner.

DON'T JUDGE A BOOK BY ITS COVER

Kevin had described himself as a "chicken catcher" from rural Kentucky when he came onstage for his original audition. The judges appeared ready to mock him. Backstage, Cannon made fun of Kevin's thick southern accent. As the singer answered questions, members of the audience giggled.

But from the moment Skinner began singing Garth Brooks's "If Tomorrow Never Comes," a hush settled over the audience. The only sounds were Skinner's voice and guitar. As he sang the final notes, the audience was on its feet, cheering and applauding. Piers Morgan summed up the reaction:

> "There's a moment in every season—I can remember them all—
> when somebody comes on stage, dressed like you are, and your
> cap's on the wrong way 'round, and you know, this is going to
> be a total car crash. And then you start to sing and within about
> 20 seconds you had me. And by the end of it that was one of the
> most emotional, powerful performances I've seen in a long time."

"America deserves to see you," David Hasselhoff added. "You're what this show is all about."

From that moment, Skinner was marked as one of the favorites. Osbourne discussed his appeal with *People* magazine, saying that

> "It's just such a feel-good story that people just want him to win
> because he's the everyman. He's the underdog. All his life he's
> been the underdog. . . . He's so genuine, what you see is what

you get. He's not contrived, and so many people that come on this show kind of get sophisticated and they know how to play the game."

Kevin did nothing to lessen his momentum in the subsequent rounds. Recalling his feelings when he was named the winner, he told *People* magazine:

"I had never experienced anything like that and probably never will again, I would say, that dramatic. It's just the greatest feeling. I'm 35, so I have been chasing the dream for the while, and it hasn't come true. Now it's more than words can explain."

Howie Mandel

Howie Mandel was born in Toronto, Canada on November 29, 1955. After selling carpets for a while, he became a standup comic in his home town. His big break came during a trip to Los Angeles in 1979 when he went to a comedy club on amateur night. His friends told him to do a set. A producer saw him and signed him to appear on *Make Me Laugh*, a comedy game show. Eventually that led to a six-year stint on the award-winning TV series *St. Elsewhere*.

Since then he has become one of the most versatile performers in show business, appearing in an especially wide variety of television programs, game shows, movies and talk shows. One of his most notable accomplishments was creating, producing and starring in *Bobby's World*, an Emmy-nominated children's series that ran for eight seasons on the Fox Network.

Many people are struck by Howie's distinctive bald head. It is a reflection of a condition called mysophobia, or fear of germs. Howie says he feels cleaner with a shaved head. He won't shake hands with people unless he's wearing latex gloves. He prefers fist bumps. He also suffers from attentive deficit hyperactive disorder (ADHD), and spends many hours raising public awareness of the condition and how to deal with it.

ANOTHER CHANGE

Several months after the fourth season ended, another big change was announced for *America's Got Talent*. On January 6, 2010, David Hasselhoff announced that he was leaving the show to pursue the development of his own show.

Four days later, comedian Howie Mandel was tabbed to replace David on the judging panel. Mandel is perhaps best known for serving as host of the game show *Deal or No Deal*, in which contestants tried to guess which of 30 suitcases held a grand prize. Several times during the elimination process, a "banker" offered the contestant a sum of money, based on the value of the unopened cases. The contestant could take the "deal" or take his or her chances with the remaining cases.

After four successful seasons on the air, *America's Got Talent* is clearly established enough to survive changes in the cast. In fact, the program's success in the United States has inspired the creation of similar shows in other countries. And like the original program, these international versions of *Got Talent* have found a number of up-and-coming stars.

6

Scottish singer Susan Boyle attracted international attention when she appeared on *Britain's Got Talent* in April 2009. Susan surprised the judges and audience with her powerful voice. Her first album was a huge success, selling more than 8.5 million copies since it was released in November 2009.

AGT Goes Worldwide

With the success of *America's Got Talent*, Simon Cowell wanted to launch a version of the show in the United Kingdom. He signed Anthony McPartlin and Declan Donnelly to serve as hosts. Known as Ant and Dec from the first three letters of their first names, the two men were born within two months of each other in 1975. They had become friends when they appeared in the UK television series *Byker Grove* in 1989. After a successful joint singing career in the 1990s, Ant and Dec began hosting numerous television shows. One of these was *Pop Idol,* the British show that inspired *American Idol.*

Joining Simon and Piers Morgan as judges was Amanda Holden. She is a well-known British actress who has appeared in numerous stage, movie and television productions. The winner would receive £100,000 (the equivalent of about $160,000) and have the opportunity to perform at the Royal Variety Performance before members of the British royal family.

British actress Amanda Holden joined Simon and Piers on the panel of judges for *Britain's Got Talent*.

The first season was presented in a very tight format, beginning on June 9, 2007, and airing every night through the finals on June 17.

The winner was opera singer Paul Potts. Bullied as a child, Potts began singing in his school choir to get away from his tormentors. He grew up without much self-confidence and had several medical problems. Even though he spent thousands of dollars on singing lessons and appeared in several amateur operas, no agents were interested in him. He was working as a cell phone company manager and was deeply in debt when he saw an ad for *Britain's Got Talent*. Still not sure of himself, he flipped a coin to decide whether to enter.

Although the coin came up the right way, his problems weren't over on the night of his audition. As he explained,

> "When I stepped on to the stage the crowd were baying for blood. The act before had been a disaster. As I walked to the mark, in my [inexpensive] suit, I just wanted to turn around and run away."

He nailed his performance of "Nessun Dorma" that night, and sang even better in the semi-finals and finals. Since winning the show, Potts has achieved international fame. His victory led to a chart-topping album, *One Chance*, that has sold more than 4 million copies.

Sixteen-year-old street dancer George Sampson won the competition in 2008, when *Britain's Got Talent* ran for seven weeks. It began in mid-April, with the finals on May 31. Though George released a DVD and appeared in a successful musical after his victory, his career didn't take off in the same way that Paul Potts's had.

AN INCREDIBLE AUDITION

The third season of *Britain's Got Talent* aired in April 2009. It featured what would become one of the most famous moments in the history of reality television. When Susan Boyle walked onstage for her audition, the judges had low expectations. Susan was a frumpy-looking woman in her late 40s. Before performing, she told Ant and Dec, "I live alone with my cat Pebbles. I've never been kissed." When Susan told Simon Cowell

Opera singer Paul Potts promotes his first album, *One Chance*, at a 2007 event. Earlier that year, Paul had won the first season of *Britain's Got Talent*.

that she hoped to be as successful as Elaine Paige, the judges and audience members rolled their eyes. Paige, an award-winning singer and actress, is often referred to as the First Lady of British musical theatre. She has sold millions of albums. Susan, on the other hand, did not seem like she had any particular talent.

But when Susan opened her mouth and began singing, the sneers and jeers turned to cheers. For her audition, Susan sang "I Dreamed a Dream," from the musical *Les Misérables*. By the time she had finished the first line, the audience had erupted with cheers and clapping. Soon many audience members were on their feet applauding her performance. The three judges' faces were wreathed in smiles.

When Susan finished singing, she began walking offstage. The judges quickly summoned her back. The often-crusty Piers Morgan told her,

"Without a doubt, that was the biggest surprise I have had in three years of the show. When you stood there with that cheeky grin and said, 'I — I want to be like Elaine Paige,' everyone was laughing at you. No one is laughing now. That was—stunning, an incredible performance."

Amanda Holden added, "I am so thrilled because I know that everybody was against you. I honestly think that we were all being very cynical and I think that's the biggest wakeup call ever." All three judges voted to advance her on the show.

SURPRISE SENSATION

Within hours, Susan Boyle became an Internet sensation. A video of her performance was posted to YouTube.com. It soon became one of the most popular videos on the channel. Within three days, the YouTube video had been viewed more than 2.5 million times. To date, videos of

Susan Boyle's appearance on *Britain's Got Talent* became an Internet sensation. Millions of people have watched her initial performance on the Web.

her audition performance have been watched more than 325 million times by people all over the world.

Susan reached the finals of *Britain's Got Talent*, but in one of the greatest upsets in reality television history, she did not win the competition. That honor went to a street dancing group called Diversity, whose members ranged in age from 12 to 26.

The loss was barely a speed bump on Susan's road to success, though. Her first CD, *I Dreamed A Dream*, was released in November 2009. It sold more than 3 million copies in a few weeks. In December 2009 she appeared in a concert with her idol, Elaine Paige.

TALENT AROUND THE WORLD

The success of the *Got Talent* programs in the United States and United Kingdom has led to spinoffs that have aired in more than 30 other coun-

Fast Fact

Susan Boyle gave up singing for a while after her mother died in 2007. However, she decided to try out for *Britain's Got Talent* when she learned that regional auditions would be held near her home. "[My mother] was the one who said I should enter *Britain's Got Talent*," Susan later told a British newspaper. "We used to watch it together. She thought I would win."

tries. Some people say that *Got Talent* is the world's fastest-growing reality franchise, though in quite a few cases the actual name of the show has been changed. Examples include *Who Is the Star?* (Mexico), *A Star Will Be Born* (Hungary), *It's Showtime* (Austria), *A Minute of Fame* (Russia), *The Supertalent* (Germany), *Everyone Is Talented* (China), and *What Is Your Talent?* (Brazil).

One of the most famous winners of these international shows is Ukraine's Kseniya Simonova. In 2009, her remarkable eight-minute-long "sand animation" hauntingly evoked Germany's brutal invasion of her native country during World War II. During her performance, she continually rearranged sand on a light table to depict the horrors of war. Like Susan Boyle, Kseniya became a YouTube sensation.

Due to the success of these spinoffs, tentative plans have been made for a show called *World's Got Talent*. The show will feature 25 winners from various international *Got Talent* programs. There will be five or six judges, probably from the United States, Great Britain, and Australia. The overall champion will take home a million dollars.

Fast Fact

The first three winners in *Australia's Got Talent* were all young people: 12-year-old country singer Bonnie Anderson (2007), 16-year old-guitarist Smokin' Joe Robinson (2008), and 15-year-old opera singer Mark Vincent (2009).

A one night mini-version of the projected series was shown on the British network ITV in early February 2008. Piers Morgan was the host.

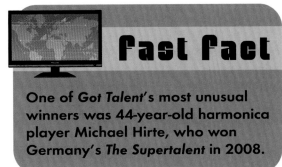

Fast Fact

One of *Got Talent*'s most unusual winners was 44-year-old harmonica player Michael Hirte, who won Germany's *The Supertalent* in 2008.

WHAT THE SHOW MEANS

No matter where a *Got Talent* spinoff airs, the message remains the same: discovering talent that probably would not have been recognized otherwise. Terry Fator is a perfect example. As he told the *Richmond Times-Dispatch*,

> "I never would have been discovered without the show because I had been knocking on doors and begging and doing everything I could and I couldn't get anyone to look at me."

Neal Boyd adds, "Moving forward, my goal is that my voice and my own story help people realize that if they work hard enough, they can realize their own dreams. I'm lucky enough that now I can reach people across the country and across the world with this message: we can achieve anything."

That message is likely to resonate with both the contestants on *America's Got Talent* and the millions of people who are the show's devoted fans.

Chronology

1934: *Major Bowes Amateur Hour* makes its debut on WFN Radio in New York City.

1948: *Major Bowes Amateur Hour* and *The Ed Sullivan Show* begin appearing on television.

1976: *The Gong Show* premieres.

1992: The *New Original Amateur Hour* debuts on Family Channel with Willard Scott as host.

2002: *American Idol* premieres.

2006: *America's Got Talent* makes its debut on the NBC Network; 11-year-old singer Bianca Ryan is the first winner.

2007: Ventriloquist Terry Fator wins the second season of *America's Got Talent.*

2008: Opera singer Neal Boyd is the winner on the third season of *America's Got Talent.*

2009: Country singer Kevin Skinner wins the fourth season of *America's Got Talent.*

2010: David Hasselhoff says he will leave the show on January 6. Four days later, Howie Mandel is announced as his replacement on the judging panel.

Glossary

amenities—elements or services that provide comfort, convenience, or enjoyment.

aria—a solo song in an opera, written to showcase the singer's vocal ability.

coveted—wanted very much.

honing—sharpening, making better.

memoirs—books that contain personal stories about the authors.

mime—performer who remains silent during his or her act, using gestures and actions in place of words.

quintet—group of five.

rendition—performance.

self-effacing—humble, modest.

ventriloquist—person who "throws" his voice onto a puppet he is holding, so that the puppet appears to be speaking.

winnowed—removed, narrowed down.

Resources

FURTHER READING

Fator, Terry. *Who's the Dummy Now?: Winner of America's Got Talent.* Chatswood, Australia: New Holland Publishing Australia Pty Ltd, 2008.

Hasselhoff, David. *Don't Hassel the Hoff.* New York: Thomas Dunne Books, 2007.

Osbourne, Sharon. *Sharon Osbourne Survivor: My Story—The Next Chapter.* New York: Little, Brown Book Group, 2009.

Whiting, Jim. *American Idol Judges.* Broomall, Pennsylvania: Mason Crest, 2009.

INTERNET RESOURCES

http://www.nbc.com/americas-got-talent/

Official website of *America's Got Talent,* with video clips, interviews, news, photos, episode guides, and more.

www.biancaryan.com

Bianca Ryan's official website, with news, clips, forum and more.

http://www.terryfator.com/

Terry Fator's official website, with news, photos, videos, blog, and store.

http://www.nealeboyd.com/

Neal Boyd's official website includes a schedule of upcoming appearances, along with his bio, news, and chats.

http://www.kevinskinnertheofficialsite.com/

The official Kevin Skinner website includes a bio, clips, merchandise, and other links.

http://www.susanboylemusic.com/gb/music

Official Susan Boyle website, with recordings, photos, news and more.

Numbers in ***bold italics*** refer to captions.

JIM WHITING has written more than 100 non-fiction books for children, and has edited over 150 more during an especially diverse writing career. He published *Northwest Runner* magazine for more than 17 years. His other credits include advising a national award-winning high school newspaper, working as sports editor for the *Bainbridge Island Review*, event and venue writeups and photography for America Online, articles in dozens of magazines, light verse in the *Saturday Evening Post*, the first piece of original fiction to appear in *Runner's World*, and official photographer for the Antarctica Marathon.